THE CLOTHES-PROP MAN

Martin R. Johnson was born at Gawler, north-east of
Adelaide, in 1950. The first 12 years of his life were
spent growing up at the married workmen's camp at
nearby Humbug Scrub, during the building of the
South Para Reservoir.

Located approximately 40 kilometres north-east of
Adelaide, this was South Australia's largest water
catchment project. Work completing the construction
of the outlet tower, spillway and dam wall lasted from
1948 until 1958.

Up to 200 workmen lived at the construction site
in small corrugated iron huts. These men were a
mixture of immigrants displaced from Europe after
World War II, others described as "vagrants loitering
about the streets of Adelaide", and men from Yatala
Labour Prison.

The Clothes-prop Man celebrates the working-class
lifestyles of these people.

BOOKS BY THE SAME AUTHOR

Non-fiction

A kind of madness – an anecdotal history of timber felling at Mount Crawford Forest, 1929–1986

Twenty Houses – an anecdotal history of the building of the South Para Reservoir, 1948–1958

Poetry

After the Axe-Men: poems from Mount Crawford Forest

As editor

The Colonial Athens. A Gawler Book of Poetry Celebrating 100 Years of Federation 1901–2001

THE
CLOTHES-PROP
MAN

Poems from the South Para Reservoir

Martin R. Johnson

**Wakefield
Press**

Wakefield Press
17 Rundle Street
Kent Town
South Australia 5071

First published 2002

Cover photographs courtesy of Williamstown Medical Clinic, *Advertiser*,
    South Australian Water Corporation
Cover design by Liz Nicholson, design BITE
Text designed and typeset by Gina Inverarity
Printed and bound by Hyde Park Press, Adelaide

National Library of Australia
Cataloguing-in-publication entry

Johnson, Martin R.
The clothes-prop man: poems from the South Para Reservoir.

ISBN 1 86254 572 3

I. Title.

A821.4

  Promotion of this book has been assisted
by the South Australian Government
Government of South Australia A R T S A through Arts South Australia.

 Publication of this book was assisted by the
Commonwealth Government through the
Australia Council, its arts funding and advisory body.

For Cathy, Marty, Vincent, Daniel & Tim

CONTENTS

Acknowledgements . . . . *x*

ONE: BUILDING THE RESERVOIR

Sack-em Jack 3
The man who played piccolo 4
Girl in a photograph 5
New Australian 6
Crossing the line 7
Spillway 9
Crusher 10
From the Cook House 12
Kitchen hand 13
The surveyor 14
A quiet bloke 15
Truck driver 16
Powder-monkey 18
Moon man 20
Folk tale poem 22
Obelisk 24
Yarns, facts or rumours 25

TWO: MARRIED WORKMEN'S CAMP

Wind 28
Aquarium 29
"I can say 30
The naturalist 31
". . . seemed all I did was have kids . . ." 32
Home (workcamp) birth 33

"All I grabbed was the baby, and the money" 35
". . . there wasn't anywhere to go, or . . ." 36
Wood 38
Bread 39
Meat 40
Milk 41
Mushrooms 43
Dog season 45
Whiskey 46
Bed time stories 47
The Chocolate-frog man 48
Pleurisy 49
Scones 50
Flames & Electrodes 51
TV 53
Cracker night 54
When Dad took the pledge 55
Dozer driver 57
The Clothes-prop man 58
Making the myth 59
In the custom of 60
Edmond & Maruta Sudrabs 61
Toboganning 63
Travelling salesman 64
Wongalere 65
Friday October 17, 1958 67
Moving 68
Trucks 70

THREE: WILLIAMSTOWN

Williamstown 72
Wrestling 74
Skid kids 75
In the character of a country town 76
Digger 77
The snake 78
George 79
Firefighters 80
Cracking almonds 81
Mrs. A 82
Mr. B 83
Mr. L 84
For the butcher 85
In the back room at Norm's 86
Forest worker 88
Vic 89
When Murray whistled 90
First love 91
For PG 92
"Squasha" 93
At the pin-ball parlour 95
Picking grapes 96
Milking cows 97
Forking silage 98
1966. with a pocketful of dollars and cents...........99

ACKNOWLEDGEMENTS

The Bunyip; The Australian; The Sydney Morning Herald; The Newcastle Herald; Antipodes USA; ABC "A First Hearing"; LiNQ; Radio 5 UV; Studio; The Western Review; Northern Perspective; Westerly; Tamba; Ulitarra; Anthology "Come down the lane with me"; Micropress N.Z.; Centoria; SideWaLK; Muse; Redoubt; Hobo; Cordite; Four W; Centoria.

Special thanks goes to Cathy Young, whose encouragement and editing advice has contributed greatly to this publication.

I also wish to express my gratitude to the workers and their families whose stories inspired some of these poems.

The writing of these poems was assisted by the Commonwealth Government through the Australia Council, its arts funding and advisory body.

ONE

BUILDING
THE
RESERVOIR

Sack-em Jack

"When you've got a big mob of men,
with a mixture of new Australians, and men
from Yatala Labour Prison, others described
as 'vagrants found loitering about the streets'
you have to make sure the work is done."

Jack was the general foreman
directly responsible to the resident engineer.
A wiry, tall and tough-as-boot leather
individual with ice inside his veins. The cool
gaze of his eye could outstare the eye
of a needle. His tongue matched its keen point.

No-one dared take on the boney shapes
of his nose and knuckles. Jawbone set
like a tyretread in cement. Men hissed his approach.
Cursed him out of earshot. Muscles oiled with
self-confidence, senses sharp as the crack of a whip,
Jack could sack a bloke easy as it is to spit.

Which suited the men avoiding maintenance, or
who were in trouble with the police. "It made
no difference to me," said Jack. "If a man
worked fair enough, I'd let him go." Just
makes you wonder how many workers' names
were Smith, or Jones?

The man who played piccolo

I have a dilemma.
A wish to write a poem inspired
by a man who I've never met.
Who played music the kind that gives
sorrow the flick. Shapes a smile
with your lips in-site-of
fingertips smashed out-of-shape
by the nazis.

She rested in the comfort of
her easy chair, the memory as fresh
in her mind as the day she
welcomed him, together with his
Czech and Polish friends, into
her home. Sung songs round her piano.
"It was a great joy to them," she said,
concluding her story.

I put down my pen and crumple
the paper. To write from hearsay
is beyond my ability. I cannot
conjure up those notes, nor construct
an image of those terrible fingers.
Club-footed forms that skipped
over the holes in his pipe
with such pleasure and agility.

Girl in a photograph

Her name is Veronica. Polish
by birth. About 15 when the shutter
of the camera caught her in front of
the corrugated iron house she shared
with four other young women.
Kitchen-hands at the camp.

She is dancing in the dirt, dressed
in a cotton frock buttoned down
the front. Her bare left foot is suspended in the air,
her body's weight balanced on the ball
of her right. Both hands' fingers are
open, level with her hips,
her arms out wide from her sides,
bent left knee and turned left shoulder
nearest the camera's lens.

But it's her face that captures
the viewer's eye. Plain as a bucket
there's a vitality in her smile
you can't describe. Reaches
inside and touches your heart.

New Australian

His straw mattress sagged
in the army surplus cot.
Voice muttered against the cold,
let in through black tar paper
lining the hut's corrugated iron walls.
Against the lack of a power point,
no plug for a heater. No ceiling either,
a single light bulb suspended from a rafter.

Nothing but his own disposition
to dispel, or add to the unfriendly
atmosphere, he was one of 200 men
surrounded by a high barbed wire fence,
their uncertainty, dread and desire
loaded aboard the backs of trucks
and driven down gullies choked with scrub.

Across stoney ridges to where pick handles
and axe-blades made ordinary workers, ex-
convicts and immigrants equal. Jarred laughter
and curses out stubborn throats.

Wet with rain, or sweaty with heat, these men
loved and hated the job. Each other
and the men in charge, or driving machines.
A time that now rests easy on their minds.
Brings to their families a sense of pride.

Crossing the line

". . . the migrant workers were very lonely. We
weren't supposed to fraternise with them. Have
them in our homes, or to visit them. One day we
brought my brother-in-law's baby into the huts to
show them. It brought back memories of their own
families. To hold a baby in their arms was a real
delight for them." Pearl Sires.

I was raised with the balts.
Eyties, huns and names I didn't understand,
living just up the road. Some were friends
of my father. Had played darts inside
our kitchen after the pub shut
on Friday nights.

Yet I can remember the collective
resentment. The warnings to us children
to keep away from their camp. Never
to go near their huts. To run
inside if we saw one of them walking
down the road.

Fifty years later her telling me her offer
of friendship and hope
has opened my mind like that gate
with water splashing in puddles
under the wheels of yesterday's tyres.

I imagine a sky heavy with clouds; sound
of the car door, a woman hurrying across
the compound dressed in a woollen overcoat,
bright scarf in the wind about her hair.
A baby in her arms, wrapped up in a shawl
crocheted by her mother. The step outside
the hut is trampled and muddied.

The air inside, cold and pungent
with the odour of men. Stale smoke of cigarettes.
A man starts at this unexpected intrusion,
his eyes glazed over with inner concerns
we can never know. Swings his legs
over the edge of his cot, and takes
the bundle gently in his hands.

I listen to her tell me the story, and
something of what this man had felt
 weighs in my own arms.

Spillway

"We were living right on the site. We could hear it,
see it and smell it constantly. I felt more involved
with that construction project than any other," said
the wife of the resident engineer.

A man who men still speak of
in a he-was-a-good-bloke tone
of voice which causes his presence to loom
somewhat romantically in our minds.

Tamper with the bias bosses are
bosses and that's all a workman's
disposition allows. That
he was a man who saw futures
and meanings in backs bent across
surveyed lines.

Workers whose hands had been bloodied
and blistered by the job, where
concrete now seals the hardness of
shoveled dirt and stones.

Crusher

"Sweat was running out our bootlaces"

For Bert

He was sitting in his ute
next to the wood heap
in the back yard, the sun
keeping him warm through
the windscreen;
stranglehold emphysema had
on his lungs turning
his laughter to
a painful cough, remembering
the hot nights
carting rock to the crusher.

Easy for me to see him, cigarette
at a jaunty angle to his mouth,
face and body wet with sweat, the fat
exhaust of the Eucla blasting heat
inside the truck's cabin – larrikin
attitude in the way he swung
the steering wheel. Though now
it's his contempt for the loss
of his former strength
that hardens the line of his mouth.
Accepts the inevitabilities.

I'd known him since I was a boy.
The barman at the pub
where I drink told me he'd died
two weeks after the funeral.
A month since we last shook hands.
My fingers shaking as I reached
for the glass on the bar.

From the Cook House

At night, after work, when idleness
fidgets with the minds of men with only
men for company, mostly strangers, themselves
occupied with alienation, isolation, or, in
simpler, less stressful terms, bored to
bloody-mindedness, no familiar voice
on the telephone to ring, weekend lookforwardness
outside the camp, the cook emptied the empty
Saturday night mess hall of its darkness. Shoved
familiarity up against the walls with the colours
and rustles of women's clothes. Shooed
lethargy out the room with the sounds of a
piano, accordion and violin – feet that danced
across bright floorboards. Morale a gate-crasher
that slid through the sawdust like men
with wings on their heels.

Kitchen hand

This side the bay marie, single, young, she
eyed his European handsomeness and sensed more
than a knot of hunger begin to tighten in
   his stomach,
his thoughts climbing the barbed wire at night to
inside the house she shared with the other women,
her own desires adrift in the moonbeams
moving across the floor.

Married now, they reminisce with happy
cheerful faces, his voice still heavy with
accent; her's incurably Australian. Lives met
and twined around a history of dam building and
pipelines. Work camps strong with cookhouse smells.
Memories of the South Para.

A world which existed only in the gleam of
each other's eyes. Warmth of their laughter.
Fingers that reached out to join hands with
the touch that lasts forever.

The surveyor

"This is what we call
a lazy wind. It goes straight through you . . ."

Of course, no bones tinkled like the bars
of a xylophone, huddled round
a 44 gallon drum roaring flames and sparks,
morning this line was first heard,
retrieved from fifty years ago by the Yank
made a china plate by men with lingo
that dinkumned him Australian. Cool dude
to you, now these quaint terms have fallen
more than just a tad behind today's
happenings. Culture inventing and re-inventing
itself out of a continuum of free expression.
Words that weave in and out our subconsciousnesses,
mannerisms and sensitivities, giving us
a collective sense of identity. Like these men, backs
turned to the drum of burning wood, light drizzle
staining their hats and coats, early-morning mist
blowing out over the hills and scrub, towards where
they strode in typical good humour, the Yank
lost in a trail of wit dry as the mud
of a dam in summer. Legs of his theodolite
caught in the cracks as he put his eye
to the glass. Sighted his own absence
among the rocks and trees.

A quiet bloke

He arrived on the bus
one cold dry night
dressed in a thin shirt
and worn grey trousers.
Under his arm
was a blanket wrapped in newspaper.

The usual bets were made
on how long he'd last
until, after six weeks
working the pick and shovel
like he was three men,
they relented.

He was a quiet bloke
and kept to himself
but the boss,
with the intention of helping him,
couldn't help asking
why he refused overtime?

"I work five days a week
for the bookies and publicans,"
he declared.
"I'm not going to work six."

Truck driver

"My Fargo tipper was the only truck
on the site to begin with," he said. "I got
free petrol, and was paid extra for the truck.
The money came in real handy, especially since
I was trying to raise nine kids."

Nine kids! Now that's what you'd call a real
incentive to get out of bed each morning.
Pull on the boots and get a good belly full
of tucker. Leave for work with a thermos primed
with hot tea. And, for that matter, sangas with
the kind of filling that'd pull you through
the toughest day.

I can see him now, kitbag in one hand,
the other wrenching open the truck's door,
bawl of babies a dull ache in his ears,
mobility of his legs, arms and mind
fudged by lack of sleep.

Yet his sense of responsibility pulls him inside the cabin.
The sound of the truck's motor coming on echoes out
across the dew wet paddocks, giving voice
to the family's sense of security. Twin yellow
headlight beams stab the early-morning darkness
as he thumps the cabin door shut. Clatters the gears
and releases the clutch, the Fargo's nose turning in
to the sandy track that leads away from the front
of the house.

He reaches for the rag on the dash. Wipes the fog
of his hot breath from the windscreen glass. Focuses
his eyes on familiar roadside scenes. Guns
the motor toward the dawn lighting up the hills.
Ideals and a way of life that shaped
the history of the State in the grip
of his fingers on the steering wheel.

Powder-monkey

For Luigi

He arrived from Italy in 1952.
Twenty years old with "Just enough
English to get by." Started work
at the reservoir in 1955. Was
nationalised in Williamstown in 1956.

I arrived outside his house one
sunny afternoon in 1992. I knew it
was his place before I spotted
the number, his son with a bucket
of soapy water, washing his monaro
in the drive.

Still with the water works after
37 years, he shook my hand
with pride. Proudly introduced me to
his wife and family. The good mate
who lived next door.

Even then, before I could start
the interview, he had to show me
the veggie garden. Explain the tomatoes,
cucumbers and zucchini. Open
a bottle of beer.

"I was in charge of a group
of Greek men," he said, explaining
the detonation pattern he used to blast
the spillway into shape. "I couldn't
speak Greek, and they couldn't understand
me."

Ten men drilling holes to lay 200
charges of gelignite, hooked up to a
main lead 500 feet long, the whole
show orchestrated by the
universal language of waving hands.
Shaking and nodding heads. Later,

in the spring, for only the
second time, the reservoir flooded
down the spillway. And as I watched
the foamy lace-like patterns
the water made, spilling out across
the concrete face, I thought of Luigi
and his men.

And for a moment felt the shudder
of exploding earth under my feet,
like the first time they set foot
on Australian soil.

Moon man

"Moon man reckoned there were women in space 100s of
years old, and one day would come down and sort us out."

Had a star tapped his shoulder
dead of night with the moon
perfectly round and still, and lips
older than the world, and womanly,
whispered their secrets to his soul?

In the reality of camp life he
scrubbed clean the ablutions block.
Emptied rubbish bins outside
the huts. Provided the men
with comic relief.

"One night a bloke dressed
in a diver's suit, complete with
brass helmet and flippers, knocked
at his door. 'I told you
they'd be down' moon man said."

Unbolting his helmet, the joker
and his mates went off to bed.
Not fooled for a minute,
moon man stretched out
with a smile the length of his mouth.

Like comets streaming across a night sky
galaxies of possibilities lit up
the universe inside his mind.
And something warm touched his cheek,
soft as breath.

Folk tale poem

The Outlet Tower, of the "dry" type, is 51.2ms high.
Water can be drawn from five different levels, ensuring
only the best quality water is released down stream to
the Barossa reservoir. The outlet tunnel is about
228ms long and 6.7ms high.

With just a rolly-weed paper gap between
two passing Euclid trucks, one tray empty, the other
filled with rock, their tyres splashing
in the watered-down dust, motors roaring powerfully,
the tunnel inched its way through the hillside's base.

Was blasted into its circular shape by a "French mob
called Etudes," pumping concrete in behind a
steel 'form-work frame,' until the racket of
machinery and men became gaping Os
of silence at the tunnel's ends.

Gathered inside the control room
to witness the first opening of the valves,
senior staff saw the view outside the port-holes
change. Felt the tower shudder
and begin to sway.

"They sent two of us up inside the tunnel
in a row boat to alter the outlet pipe.
It was pitch black, apart from our torch beams."
A working life recollection remade as folklore.
A poem to float through the water mains.

Obelisk

"By the grace of God
Mid much despair,
We built this dam
        Despite
Victoria Square"
                Bill Benton

Message in an empty whiskey bottle, emptied
by men with overdue grins, strife caused by
weather, physically and mentally taxing times,
red tape setbacks in-between, smothered by
a united sense of pride.

The words "despair" and "Despite" no longer
forceful reminders, cap screwed tight the bottle
was buried within the foundation pour
of the stone pillar.

The weather vane's arrow points true north
                above
            four tapered
        walls mounted with
        brass information plates

Visitors climb steps. Consider the project.
Leave with smiles on their lips. Involuntary
chuckles of laughter. Or else with hands
inside their pockets, the words
of a simple poem a secret to them.
A grin preserved in whiskey fumes.

Yarns, facts or rumours

". . . and the storeman, Dick 'Spewey' Rogers, who
had a drinking problem – which matched the rest of
us – was usually drunk as a monkey when you went
to get something. Usually it took an hour, and a
handkerchief full of tears before you got what you
wanted."
                    Bill Forrestal

The stories I've been told . . . !

"He couldn't be bothered using a bucket
to fill the radiator. So he drove the dozer
straight into the creek. Waited til
it was full, then backed out."

Men with morning hang-overs
on such a regular basis
the first aid bloke, J. J. Fry, who doubled
as the saw doctor (he sharpened the tools
for scrub clearing), would write "hang-over"
next to a man's name suffering badly
with flu.

Saturday orders of grog
to Falkenburgs winery (between Rowland Flat
and Tanunda) that made "my Austen A40
drag on the road."

Men sacked inside the pub
during working hours, troublemakers
carted off aboard the cop's motor bike
and side-car to his "little wooden cell out
on his back lawn, big enough for two men."

On pay mornings
it took five gang trucks to transport
the men to the work-sites. But after a night
at the pub "you could take them all
in the back of a ute!"

Yarns, facts or rumours
we wrap ourselves in them
like fleecy blankets
to keep out the cold. Heritage, outrageous
or dutifully sublime, an open fire
round which we sit, our minds restless
to hear the next story told.

TWO

MARRIED
WORKMEN'S
CAMP

Wind

My mother
loves to dream
in paddocks of wind
twirling hollow logs
into outcrops of rock
and long gullies of birds
          high up
tucking in their wings
to blow away
like paper flapping down a street:

and as I turn in the womb
pressing my ear to the sound
I feel her hand
rest on my shoulder -
her eyes converging
on the distant hills
         and further . . .

Aquarium

I was born
and raised in a workmen's camp
where men carved a reservoir out of scrub and rock
with fingers fond of the feel of a bottle and neck
of a woman – the squeeze of a trigger – flashing knives
– hot blood in the chill of a morning kill

given life
by a woman still in her teens scrubbing floors
with knees that knew the long miles to town –
the weight of sick children and bottled grog along a
dirt road breathing diesel and the promise of endless
tomorrows

growing up with children
with the wind in their hair – the feel of trees in
their blood – the taste of dirt in their flesh – children
whose world began and ended where the scrub met the edge
of town – their wild innocent eyes bumping like fish
against the invisible wall of an aquarium

until the water broke through
and time hauled the out –

the sound of breaking glass forever in their hearts.

**"I can say this was one of those jobs
where a bloke'd look forward to going
to work."**

This is, of course, the voice
of a man from the married workers' site,
where twenty identical wooden transportable houses
were put up on posts to keep out the weather
and the snakes, the camp spread out along
a high ridge, separated from the scrub by a
firebreak. Gravel road outside their front gates
leading to Williamstown three miles east, the
work site of the reservoir a mile west.

Wood fire comfort, ice-boxes and a few first fridges
his life was children, pets and wireless sets. Woman
who kept his body warm at night. Had his
breakfast on the kitchen table before his feet
shoved inside his boots.

With the past and future extinquished
by her parting kiss, he lived in a continual present
without the burden of fear or hate.

The naturalist

"I never picked the wild flowers."

For her, before the invention
of nowaday's conservationist ideals
when children pressed native orchids
in books, tweesered those coloured
spiky spiders from their webs,
scorpions out under rocks to
drown in bottles of methylated spirits
to be gawked and wondered at,
the sights, smells and sounds of
the scrub out-marvelled their
physical shapes. Became irresistibly
untouchable. A carpet never to be
vacuumed. Pretty patterned tablecloth
thrown down at a picnic under the
trees – never to be shaken of crumbs.

But lift a corner . . . There,
in the darkness you'll find the wildness
that got inside her heart. The freedom
that stung her senses like thorns
on a prickle bush. What it was
she dare not meddle with.

". . . seemed all I did was have kids . . ."

In summer the washing line was
wrestled to the count of three by
a tag team of flapping legs and
arms; winter a case of
the clothes-horse not being able
to raise a gallop in the lounge,
the backs of chairs
in front of the fire, stooped
old men with sleeves down
to their knees.

At night, the house quiet with
baby breath, children's mouths
dribbling spit into their pillows,
snores in the passage-way
of her husband's nostrils,
she slept warm with her dreams.

Belly swelling
with the fifth child, she
gathered the walls of her house
about her shoulders
like a shawl. Busied her fingers
knitting and cooking meals.
The bawling and laughter
of her young; her life, her
breath, her world.

Home (workcamp) birth

What he'd do for a drink!

Neither her nor the car
were certain to make it,
12 miles to the hospital further
than 12 miles today.

Besides, his nerves had bolted . . .
Shut him out the room,
his bottle of port stranded
next to the bed.

Requests for hot water
filling his mind and the kitchen
with scalding steam, as he stoked the fire
like a boiler in a train.

When the midwife insisted
he witness the birth, panic
galloped about in his head
like a mad horse.

Their daughter going warm and
sticky into her mother's arms.
His bottle slipping between
his fumbling fingers.

The moment lost to the
inevitabilities. Clean sheets
for the bed. Saucepans rescued
from the stove.

Midwife's shoes
fading from the driveway stones.

"All I grabbed was the baby, and the money"

Survival instincts, no doubt.
Automatic actions against the
threat of bushfire. At least
should the night end here
in complete ruins, there'd be
dough to buy a feed. Family
name'd live on . . .

In any case, there she
and others like her were, sons
and daughters; babies aboard
comfortable hips out in front
of front gates, hair tangled
by sleep, hearts panicky
in their chests.

Though no truck was ever sent,
her head returned to the pillow,
an image of her standing outside
by the gate post remained. Stood stockstill
and resolute, all through the dawn
and on into the next, and
the next, and next . . .

". . . there wasn't anywhere to go, or anything else to do. Nothing for the women to get involved in. Even the works social club was organised for us."

Surrounded by scrub:
she made her escape
in the serials broadcast
on the radio . . .

Marriage and rag
she used to polish
the linoleum; daytime games
of cards with other women
who shared this 50s
working-class tradition.

Men arriving home
in the back of the work truck,
big calloused hands, kissing
bewiskered lips; clothes and skin
smelling of sweat, dust & diesel . . .

Children home from school
in the back of a red Bedford truck.

Women confined to the family
home, their sense of
frustration and under-achievement
concerns that oiled the blocks
& tackles of 60s change.

A transition I grew up with.
Kangaroos crossing the fire break
in the evening light. Night sounds
of the scrub in our ears
as we lay in our beds
easy with sleep.

Wood

"It was 16 years before I was game
enough to switch an electric oven on."

Old memories flared in her eyes
like newspaper poked in under
kindling, and set on fire.

Returned her thoughts to the scrub
and those splintery chunks
of split red gum.

To the smell of cooking from the
old wood stove; a roast in the oven,
heat of burning wood
through the iron grate.

Hot yellow tongues of flame
that spoke to her the language
of security.

Even now, when she switches on
the electric stove, wood whispers
to her in the red coils
of the plate.

Bread

Come for a drive with M
when he switched his thoughts
from the back of Hodson's bakery
to the workers, camped just out of town.

Consider what you'd make of
the bumpy dirt road full of rumours
the likes of, "There's only criminals
out there!" in reference to the men
who lived in the single workers' huts.

Hand the married women their orders; hot
loaves wrapped in white tissue paper. Women
in dresses cut to below their knees,
paying in shillings & pence.
Women come outside their homes
at the sound of the van's approach,
disappeared now from this setting
of native scrub. A way of life
replaced by a NO TRESPASSING sign:

Two miles from the nearest shops
at Williamstown, the married workers
and their families, the single and
alone lived in a kind of obscurity.
Were a kind of mystery.

Turned the eyes and lowered
the voices of townsfolk
when one of us entered the street.

Meat

Not the slaughterhouse kind, tame
cuts on hooks in the back
of the butcher's van. We hungered
for the hunt. Taste of game.

Fingers red with blood,
the smell of the kill
inspired in us a kind of
savagery.

Surrounded by scrub, we weren't
confined by townee ideals.
The knots we used to tie
fish-hooks, setting loose
our sense of freedom.

A bullet fired straight through
an animal's beating heart,
a near-enough interpretation
of reality.

In the light of the fireplace,
bellies gone round and warm,
we picked our teeth
with a clear conscience.

Tug of the moon
in the blood that pulsed
dark and hot
through our veins.

Milk

In the morning, the true morning,
before the smoke of wood fires
began to rise, milk was delivered;
ladelled from a can into the various
sized billies standing next to, or
hanging from the gate posts.
    "What's that?
    Stolen!
    Itwasn'tme."
In all seriousness, my face couldn't have
been more than an insignificant blot,
a blur or smudge barely discernible
through the dew streaks of my bedroom
window. Dew which melted on contact
as my feet skipped through the grass
reaching my knees . . . and ran away from
my fingers destroying all evidence as
I lifted each silver lid and gratefully
gathered the coins (Sometimes there'd be
a note with a note "Change, please") into
my marble tin.
    "What tin?"
And on frosty nights, which out here
started at midnight and lasted till
dinner-time, almost, inches thick, hot
like a branding iron, and as hard as
concrete, though it dented as soon as
you touched it, bare toes looked like
dog tracks – provided you kept your heel up.

*

Dumped out onto the table, the coins
flipped heads & tails of guilt and
shame through my conscience. Notes
rustled, then lay damning me with
their silence. The gaping O of the
empty tin, the mouth of treachery.
  "Alright!
  I know about the money.
  My brother did it."

Mushrooms

We believed in the elves
that sat atop their white domes
in circles on those
full moon nights, drawn out
of our warm homes and across
low hillsides, cool and green
in the autumn light; wind
in our hair, sunlight flashing
on our knives . . .

We'd walk for hours
through the damp grass, our eyes
on the lookout for mushrooms,
each discovery an exciting find.
Something ancient and tribal
pulsed through our veins . . .

When our buckets were full
we followed the track
through the scrub which led towards
our homes, greeted by the sight
and smell of woodsmoke adrift across
the iron rooftops . . .

Peeled and soaked
in salty water, a stew
of legends and myths simmered
in saucepans on our kitchen stoves . . .

Splashed steaming hot
across buttered toast we
gathered about our plates of mushrooms
like goblins in fairy tales.

Dog season

They came from nowhere.
We didn't know why.
Tall loping dogs.

Black, brindle, every colour.
Pink tongues hanging out
come to visit our bitch.

"Mum, come quick,"
I remember yelling.
"The dogs' bums are stuck!"

Mum broke them apart
with a stick, the dogs scattering
to stand a short way off.

Only to come slinking back,
snarling and erupting into fights
that drew blood from savage bites.

The air stunk of dog semen and sweat.
Dog blood and the smell of dirt.
The frenzy of a bitch on heat.

We didn't understand.
It was outside of our world.
But we liked it when Sandy had pups.

Whiskey

was a magnificent Stag Hound.
His coat was pure white and he dripped love
all over us with his huge pink tongue. Like blood
running from the throat of a sheep, killed in fun.

Mum'd wash the pointed snout and shoo
the farmer away as though he were a fly.
Whiskey was the last in a line of dogs
taken into the scrub to die.

Chained up to a tree and shot
fair between the eyes, and left to decompose
in some shallow grave, no stone or post
to remember him by.

The bullet ending the feel of his neck under
my arm; a last goodbye before I ran
to catch the bus to school. The gap
it made, an ache in my side.

Bed time stories

On Anzac day, mum told us about
the fun of air raid drills at school.

How she used to spit through the wire
at the internees camped just out of town.

And the excitement troop trains caused,
like when her friend "Hughie" left:

But when Hughie came to visit,
I couldn't match her enthusiasm.

I just stared and stared and stared
at the stump that was his leg.

The Chocolate-frog man

Sunday afternoons
I drew circles with a stick in the gravel
near the gate.
Or sat plugging ant holes
waiting with my younger brother
for him to arrive.
All at once his car would be there,
and he'd crash through the door with two paper bags
filled with chocolate-frogs.

Then his laughter would fill the house
as match sticks danced my father's crib-board
from side to side;
the flagon bottoming out
to a version of "Heart-of-my-heart . . ."
our eyes joining in.

One Sunday he didn't come.
Dad took us to a strange place
with rows of polished stones,
and stood us before a mound
of freshly-turned earth. A tin jar
filled with flowers.

Pleurisy

It was Donald Duck made dad
well again, quacking away with
Hughie, Dewie & Louie as they sped
across the countryside in their funny
car, to camp out at Yellowstone Park.

Goofy and Gyro Gearloose. Archie
and Superman. All of my comic book
heroes, brought each day on tiptoe
to the side of his bed where he lay
felled like a massive tree.

Each night I'd bring a fresh supply,
swapped for marbles and some of my
favourite toys. Comics were the best
thing to make you feel good. Forget
the bad that make you cry.

Though when mum let up the blind
and opened the curtains in dad's room,
the window letting in the air and sun,
I had to do some fancy talking
to get those comics out of his hands.

To get back the treasures I'd lost
doing deals with my friends.

Scones

We'd eat them tongue-scalding hot.
The butter boiling like a yellow pool
up on some tropical mountain slope. Steam
stinging our eyes, the crusts hard
as ground baked by summer sun.

Eat them sticky-tongue cold.
The butter congealed thick as yellow mud.
Flour gumming up our teeth, the crusts
moist from being in the fridge. Scones
wet more than our appetites.

They sat us together at the kitchen table,
our bellies round and warm. Put smiles
on our faces. Laughter in our hearts . . .
and made our hands at ease and calm.
Talk with harmony in our lives.

A mixture of flour and water
beaten flat with a rolling pin. Circles
cut with an up-turned glass. The pure heat
of an oven fuelled by wood. The care
of my mother's hands.

Flames & Electrodes

"When the men went away to the camp at Tarlee,
the first TV came to the house site. So those women
who needed company most at night would go to
watch it. Entrance Fee a stump of wood for the fire."
                    Fay Quinn

Let's face it, the sight
of flames . . . their movement
suspends your reasoning:
The sound of heat
levering apart grains of wood
clenched tight as fists tunes
the mind with imaginings. The feel
of warmth entices
a sense of security beyond
those that lie beneath
the limits of your skin.

Given over to a box
on four stumpy legs,
the flicker of black & white
images drew the women's eyes, and
captured their awareness; the sounds
of recreated life inventing
a sense of lived experience. No
pokers needed to stir
dying embers into action, this
new invention stirred
the blood inside their veins.

When it came time
to turn off the set,
the picture tube cooling
and losing the scenes, talk over
cups of tea and cake wasn't
the same. Like the red reflection
of coals inside the dull glass
from the fireplace, something
of themselves remained trapped
by the electrodes. Something wild
and daring, not giving a yelp.

TV

To think you could see as well
as hear the action . . .

Whose place it was and when
I can't remember, but that first strange
shiny aerial bolted to the roof
not only picked up televised signals,
it attracted the brain waves of kids
picking up the vibes of social change.

My brother and I used to climb
a tree and sit in the branches
that overlooked the back yard until
we got invited in, the lounge full
of kids eating biscuits and drinking
raspberry cordial. "Crusader Rabbit" "Fury"
"The Three Stooges" & "The Cisco Kid" taking
our minds on fantastic journeys.

Or else we'd climb down and trudge
home in the dark.

The wireless in the corner with
its music and commotion, suddenly
a status symbol antiquated by
moving images on glass.

The knobs and valves tuning me in
to a sense of who we were.

Cracker night

Bungers were best.
Tightly packed cartridges of gunpowder
that fired stones out pipes, blew up letter boxes, off
fingertips that held on too long.

Even flowerpots, with their eruptions of pretty
sparks, packed a real wallop. And you've never
seen a kid move so quick as when
a jumping jack chases after her, or him.

Catherine wheels spinning free of nails hammered
into posts soon got the mob outside on
the firebreak hopping. Guy Fawkes night
at the camp, the air a chaos of noise and light.

A stream of sparks trail off upwards
as my mind empties of memories. Shrieks
of fear and pleasure. Laughter that tells you
everyone's having a good time.

Now cracker night comes and the streets stay dark.
No sparks, hisses, fizzes and bangs. Sting
of burnt gunpowder in your nose and lungs. Guy
ablaze in a hill of sticks and grass.

Poking my hands deep inside my pockets
I mope down the silent street, these
thoughts an unlit fuse
in search of a match.

When Dad took the pledge

It certainly gave the family a lift.
Dad going off to the police station,
his driver's licence attained simply by
answering questions on a form (Quids
made from immigrants who couldn't read
or write, so the story goes) arriving home
in a splutter of smoke and fumes.

A plastic windowed crank start model
car that graced our driveway as surely
as if it were a brand new FJ Holden.
Dad stashed his Super Eliot bike in
the spare room while mum put on her
red dress. Washed behind the ears of
us kids.

What a mob of richos
we thought we were, the wind in our hair
as dad steered us down the bumpy
gravel road, too thrilled to sit back
in our seats, eyes seeing the view
as if for the first time.

We arrived in Williamstown right on
opening time. There's something about Saturday
morning in the front bar of a pub. The smells
and taste of raspberry is fresh, the voices
of the drinkers loud with expectation – on
this occasion the subject of motor cars.

Then it was off across the countryside to
the pub at Tungkillo, via the pub
at Mount Pleasant. We amused ourselves
as kids do till the sun went down. Till
dad staggered out and we sped out of town,
mum swallowing bex powders as dad
swerved on and off the road. Braked madly
to avoid hitting trees. Crisscrossed the white
line like the car had drunken wheels.

Our eyes were white with fright.
We had to prise our fingers loose
from the edges of our seats when, with
great gasps of relief, we arrived home
and dad swore off driving for life.

Dozer driver

The thick smell of earth and diesel
hung like incense in the air
as I clambered across the wide steel track
into my father's hands

reaching from a jumble of tall yellow levers
tangling my legs as his foot stamped
the turning brake and we squealed away toward
the cutting in the hill

where we ate lunch
and yarned like old mates
(though I rarely listened
 being too intent on my own version)

until his eyes gathered in their patience
under the rim of an army surplus cap
and the dozer blade dipped
into waves of soft brown earth

beyond the reach of the reservoir
hinting memories all in blue

The Clothes-prop man

He arrived on our back step from the scrub.
A battered hat on his weathered head.
We could smell him through the flyscreen as
he screwed his eyes
at our strange faces, peering out.
Wondering who he was?

In his hands was a wattle stick, newly skun.
Expertly shaped with a fork at the topmost end.
"Would y like a clothes-prop, missus?" he said,
jaw swivelling at the thought of food
in payment for his work.

Mum filled a paperbag with scones and fruit
while he hooked the washing line up in the wind.
Then he slung his bedroll across his shoulders
and left with the parcel in the pocket of his coat.
We followed his steps till the orange peel ran out.

Making the myth

Fridays under school age my brother
and I spent the day at the pub
with mum in Williamstown, walked in from
the camp to polish floors and silverware
that shone like the eyes of men
hearty with laughter in the afterwork hours
of the bar.

Mum'd lift us up to see dad
through the slide the women used who
drank in the lounge, others preferring husbands
to serve them outside inside their cars.
They'd beep the horn when their glasses
ran dry. I can still see those old
batwing doors crash open outwards, the hurry
in his fingers splashing a fresh supply.

At six o'clock in the early-evening, dawn
of the night's revelry, the pub shut:
my brother and I collected from the log
on the veranda, and loaded aboard
someone's headed-that-way car

the growing silence reeling away from
the front step like a drunk with two bottles
of beer in a brown paper bag. Mythology
slipping over its shoulders like a
coat, town lights bobbing like corks
from the rim of a wide-rimmed hat.

In the custom of . . .

Sunday nights the chip heater
roared an ultimatum of flames
and sparks, fuelled by the pong
of our week-old unwashed bodies.
A custom ingrained into the skin
of our way of life, like leaving
lights out till dark.

Velvet soap a conspirator,
the hot suds infiltrated our minds
with clean smells and thoughts, steam rising
from our backs
levering apart the cold air as we
stepped brand new out the bath.

The pyjamas we wore and hair
combed free of tangles, groomed
our personalities by the wireless to sing
the top 40 songs, favourites "The Flying
Purple People-Eater" and "Rock
around the Clock."

Heads gone to pillows with
the door slightly open, we'd listen to
our parents' voices come down
the passageway, the future bright
as stars through the glass of
the bedroom window. Unremembered
dreams of yesterday.

Emond & Maruta Sudrabs

Children born in Latvia, come
to live at the workmen's camp in 1950.

I never knew them, nor have we ever
met. Not even a once-off at the pub,
glasses splashing, "I'll be blowed, so this
is you!" Reunion specially planned to
celebrate these vanished years.

It's the sound of their names, whiff
of Baltic sea, old histories moored
to Riga's wharves that has me intrigued.
The splash of waves against a ship's bows
swamping their minds with uncertainty, the future
prickly as the scrub where they came to live.
Muddled as the language and customs
they didn't know.

The Latvian poet, Juris Kunnoss says,
"have no fear of the forest and its dark
sultry murmur" in his poem *One more life*.
They lived another life, here among
the sticks and stones of my own
growing up.

I move among old hedgerows, flattened lengths
of fencing wire that once divided the homes; trees
that overlooked back yards, trying to imagine
them. The sounds of their voices, colour

of their eyes, only to be drawn as always
to all that remains of the camp.

A concrete step. The empty space
where the house had stood, inhabited now
by wind and grass. Sunshine and shadows.
The evolution of the present. As I leave

the warm breath exhaled by my lungs, disperses
with night coming on.

Toboganning

When they blew up the Dutchman's house
on top of the hill above Victoria Creek,
we salvaged a sheet of roofing iron
and went sliding down through the steep
blades of grass.

One morning, the slope greased with dew,
the sheet of iron worn flat and smooth,
(*slick* would be a better term) dad
climbed aboard with a daring grin.

Free fell into the depths of our world and
became a child once more, laughing on the slope
of a hill steep with fun, the black & white football
beanie he wore, spinning like a frisbee tossed high
in the wind.

Now my sons ride the thrill
of virtual reality games, and as I grab hold
of the controls, feel a slick free fall
send a rush of blood through my heart
like iron over grass.

Travelling salesman

Was this the end of those
dusty by the side of the road
women in pinnies times? His
good-natured laugh and smile
climbed out from behind
the steering wheel of his
grey bull-nosed truck.

Cuts of cloth and baby clothes
sold with been-around ease,
he'd resume his country town
round with dust rising from
behind the wheels. Our sense
of remoteness trailing along
in the camphor smells.

A memory lost now
to the bar-coded blip
of check-out aisles.

But, hey. In these times
of economic rationalisation,
soon the week's shopping'll be
moused out on computer screens.
Delivered by the company's van.

Look! Coming up your street!
The past pulling up outside your house.

Wongalere

A cottage extensively renovated by William Gilbert.
Born at Pewsey Vale in 1887, he married Catherine
Pauline Browne in 1917. At completion the building
contained 22 rooms. The finished timbers and
stonework provided a grandeur unequalled in the
area. Inside the high water mark of the reservoir, it
was totally destroyed by 12 plugs of gelignite in
1948.

"I attended to their personal needs,"
said Jean, the Gilberts' housemaid, 1942-43,
the years drawn back like curtains when
she carried morning tea to their room,
revealing intimacies

fresh as a face splashed by cool
rainwater. Clear as the sound of a bell rung
to announce the next course of a meal. Smells
of men excused to the smoking room. Ladies
retired to the piano.

"The blast left me deaf for more than a week,"
the blaster laughed, his old fingers
tingling at the thought of those
firing leads.
                    Plunger's handle.

Exposed by lack of rain,
the homestead's magnificence is now
an impressive heap of stones. The low water
glitters in the sun. Small waves slap
against the debris.

The relic stone has no remorse.
Is an unemotional witness to the passing of time.
The lives of the family that once called this home.
Held in our hands it is our sense of loss
that weighs on our minds.

Friday October 17, 1958

Official opening of South Para Reservoir
by the Premier of SA, Sir Thomas Playford.

Like war paint on the cheek of the sky
a rainbow striped the grey rain clouds
gathering like a prophesy descending upon
the crowd of school children arrived
to witness the opening of the dam.

Dampness was on the breath of the wind
bludgeoning our hands and faces red
as it swooped in from across the valley
cleared of orchards and native scrub
to make way for the water supply.

The speeches were lost to the echoes
the microphone made as the wind whipped
the words down into the cavern of the spillway,
and up out along the gully toward
the Barossa with its "Whispering Wall".

Decorated with blue velvet curtains, the tablets
with their reservoir information were opened
at the tug of a gold cord, the Premier's fingers,
pink at the end of his suit's grey sleeve, a salute
to the workers and what they'd achieved.

Moving

We were the last family to leave.
A move we truly believed would never happen,
even though semi-trailers had been
carting the houses away for years, one by
vacated one.

We saw the empty spaces they left
behind as somewhere new to poke around.
Only when the truck drove into Williamstown,
loaded up with the last of our stuff, did we
begin to understand. The first 12 years
of a married life, wrapped in the pages of
The Women's Weekly. Memories in mum's eyes
wrapped in thin tissue paper, easily torn
and spilling tears.

Dad was heavy-handed with the past, but
every now and again he swallowed hard, the familiar
furniture out-of-place inside
these strange new rooms. Though us kids saw
the streets and nearby shops, people and houses
through eyes that convinced us this
was the only way to live.

In the late-afternoon, we walked through the scrub
for one last look at our old house.
We had no need to press our faces to the glass
of empty windows. To try the doors
like nosy parkers, eager to snoop about.

We stood a way off in the shadows
of the trees on the opposite side of the road,
yellow sun dull in the corrugations in the tin
roof. And everywhere round, a silence so still
even now it prickles my skin.

Trucks

We were hooked on the diesel fumes.
Could guess a Mac from a Euclid
by the sound, our fingers letting go
the trucks we played with in the dirt
to wave to the drivers flashing their lights.

Trucks were as much a part
of our lives as the food we ate.
When the reservoir was completed
it was strange not to hear them
thunder past our front gate.

Come up over the ridge
with birds taking flight from out
the trees, kangaroos bounding away
through the scrub, the motors loud
in our ears.

But I guess history's like that.
Roars into view tooting its horn
then overtakes the future of itself.
Becomes the present with the past
buried like tyre treads in the dust.

THREE

WILLIAMSTOWN

Williamstown, 1962

Apart from a few latest models, this
was a town with running boards on cars,
Plume petrol in their tanks. Men
riding push bikes to work through the streets,
kitbags perched between the handle bars.
Horses hitched to the water trough
across the road from the post office.

"I used to wave to the old blokes waiting
for the door to open," my uncle remembers. "Now
I'm one of them." The history of a town
recorded in worn floor boards. Counter
where arms had leaned, gossip almost obligatory
in exchange for the mail. Voices of the time
connecting people with their town.

"This was Williamstown's heyday," Laurence
Grovermann recalls, her husband Jack
Post Master then. A time when the mill yards
rang with the sounds of saw blades, filling
the streets with the smell of pine. Butcher
shops cut orders for households, straight from
the slaughter yard in the gully behind
the Methodist Church. When local dairies
delivered milk, fresh from the cow. Places
of employment after we left school.

We lived out a progression of young emotions
on the footpath in front of the post office,

waiting for "Spogs" bus to Gawler High, hormones
thumping loud through our blood.

I see us standing there still, the bus
arriving in the early-morning light. But this time
I refuse to climb aboard. I'm going fishing
for minnows in the creek. After a feed of yabbies
in the dam opposite the cemetery. Racing
down the back of George Street on my crazy go-cart.
A plank of wood with four uneven wheels, steered
by my feet, a hunk of rope in my two clenched hands.

Already I feel the corrugations jar the wheels.
Can taste the hot sweet yabby meat coming out of
the boiled red shells. Smell the fennel and hear
the water birds as the wine cork floats across
the still surface of the pool. Sense
the moment mounting when the minnow will strike . . .

The door of the bus swings open in my mind
and I see old faces go excitedly to their seats.
But for me, I'm staying here on the footpath.
This time the future can wait.

Wrestling

Sunday lunchtimes my brother and I
wrestled with dad on his big double bed.
Indian arm locks and inside step-over toe holds.
Attempts to pin down shoulders for the count
   of three!
Grunts and sweat and the feel of flesh . . .

We'd all feign sleep when mum yelled out for us to
   come and eat.
Till she banged in with the broom and swept the
   smiles off our lips.
Only we'd dive back on the bed wrestling again the
   moment she left.
One last go before the Sunday roast spoiled our fun.
You can't wrestle with a belly full of grub.

Or with a heart filled with grief.
Death put his sleeper hold on dad at age 40.
Packed the feel of his muscles and the smell of his
   skin away in a box.
Buried the passion of boys wrestling with their dad.
The memory of an arm across my throat.

Skid kids

To do a broggy
in the dirt, the back wheel
skidding out from under you
pinging stones through a cloud
of dust as your heart flies
high with exhilaration . . .

Perished tyres bandaged
with yards of green
insulation tape, tubes glued
and vulcanised so many times
they looked like round spotted snakes,
buckled wheels and bent forks,
leather shot from a seat that
bruised your delicate parts, my bike
was as close to me as my skin.

Out on my walk in the neighbourhood
where I live, black rubber marks
in the footpath skid
my feet back up on those pedals again.
Fill my nostrils with the smell of dust
as my fingers grip once more
the handlebars of my past.

In the character of a country town

The rounded balls of muscle in his arms
were as hard as the rounded ancient hills,
creases in his brow the gutters of creeks,
trees that flex in the wind his sinewy strength,
outcrops of rock his steely squint
under the weather-beaten sky of his hat,
his purpose and resolve as unshakeable as
the history that shaped the land on which
the town stands, the raised shotgun both his
privilege and right, both barrels pelting lead high
into the air with a "Take that y bastard!" shout
resonating over the Church steeple and
inside the nearby ears of the congregation
mulling over their sins outside the Church's doors,
their humility fast becoming clenched fists hustled
to kneel and pray as pigeons shat on the roof,

fingers wet with hawk's blood
turning black earth with a spade.

Digger

He lived in a tin shed
at the edge of town
ate out of cans
and slept on newspapers
packed inside thick hessian bags:

Every Friday he arrived
at 10 o'clock sharp
to empty the kerosene drum
full of shit and maggots
under the dunny seat.

He made short work of it
digging a hole in the grass
pouring filling levelling
refitting the drum with hands
suited to a job well done

like when he dug a trench at Gallipoli
and watched his mates fill it with blood;
though how could you tell
seeing him go from yard to yard
emptying dunnies five bob a drum.

A twig rustled in a nearby tree
and a bird flew into the sun:
"Nice day," I said.
"My fur coat," he replied
waving a hand between the flies.

The snake

Mum was chopping wood and the bell
was ringing "hangover music" from the tower
of Saint Peters Church when dad started screaming
for someone to bring him the axe.

He was finishing last night's flagon of plonk
watching this buxom blonde do exercises
on TV. Now here he was sounding like
he'd gone beserk.

You should've heard him in there,
screaming and banging and crashing around.
It rooted me to the spot remembering how
my mate's dad wrecked his house.

Smashed all the furniture up,
yelling and swearing drunken oaths.
Now I had that same fear in my eyes.
That same sick swirling guts.

Then the door flew open and dad
hung a dead snake on the fence, killed
by the force of his two bare feet when,
in desperation, he jumped off the couch.

George

would visit the neighbours
by walking along the tops of
their front fences. He was
always polite. "Hello," he'd say,
balancing on his way until
he'd reach the street and climb
back up the hill again.

And every afternoon
when I would be coming home
from school, he'd leap off
our gate and come running down
to greet me. "Look out!" he'd cry.
"Here comes Martin! Here comes Martin!"
climbing on top the toe of my shoe.

One morning we found him
floating face down in the copper.
Someone had forgotten to
put on the lid. None of us
heard his cries for help.
We buried him in the garden.
Should never have clipped his wings.

Firefighters

In the pub, Saturday afternoon.
The wind up and siren wailing
its story of thick brown smoke.
Flames rising up out a scrubby gully
threatening homes and livestock.

The truck pulled up to collect
volunteers, schooners of beer thrown
down throats thirsty for fun. A few
bottles scrambled on board with
drunken laughs.

But hellish flames ripping through trees
thrashing to and fro, the din and chaos
of choking smoke, flashing lights, panicky
voices on two-way radios, men deserting
hoses as trucks beat hasty retreats soon

sobered them up: Backs bruised by iron
knapsacks weighted with water, they fought
to contain the fire to the scrub as
evacuation plans for whole towns were
put in place. Ambulances and hospitals on standby.

After nine hours the rain came.
Freezing cold on the backs of their trucks
the firefighters returned to hot meals waiting
at depot sheds. Heartfelt thanks
in frying pans of eggs.

Cracking almonds

Grandmother lived at the top of Margaret Street
in a small stone cottage with an almond tree.
We used to crack the shells with a hammer on the cold
bluestone laundry floor. Chew the nutlike seeds till
our jaws ached and locked up tight.

Out of all the things we did together, like
reading books about dinosaurs, playing the
old-time wind-up record machine, pumping water
up from the underground tank, this is my most
vivid memory of her.

Down on her hands and knees, dress half-
way up her thighs, bare-footed with her eyes
wicked with delight, empty shells scattered across the floor,
the time of day set like cement against the windowpane,
the two of us forevermore.

Mrs. A

She lived next door. Hair up,
cheeky grin, eyes that flashed
good humour and spirit.

There with her hands splashing
wheat for the chooks, shifting the goat,
splitting wood and raising children.

Elbows white with flour, big floors
mopped, the smell of cooking drifting
out the windows over to our house.

In from the scrub with my traps
she always bought my rabbits,
7/6 a pair – newly skun.

Among the grass and trees, wood heap
and fowl house, she country-womanised
my ideals.

I see her still. Sometimes
in the street. Others old-time movies
on a black & white screen.

Mr. B

My ear still rings
from the clout
that sent me flying across
the front row desks.

My mouth in trouble again.
Couldn't help itself, gagged
by classroom rules when
its tongue longed to wag.

Is this why I write?
Yabber out these poems
like a factory belt
in a production line?

Some make it to print
while others return with
the ironic words "hope" & "luck"
scribbled across the rejection slip.

But critics, don't waste your time:
My teacher has rung my ear
and I've learnt to duck
that hard right hand.

Mr. L

Of all the classrooms
that I remember, how could I forget
the wind that whistled in under your door.
Wooden walls that creaked shrinking
in the bitter cold. Opened-up like ripened
pine cones in late December sun.

These were my last nib & inkwell days.
The end of blotters soaked in blue.
The grades leading from 5 – 6
when I began to make sense of the world.
When I cheated in the Friday test
so I could sit next to S.

There's no denying that you were
hard as a piece of gnarled wood
impossible to split with an axe,
but I'd give anything to come running
in from the yard and up those steps.
To sit once more at that desk.

For the butcher

I filled the steel bucket and splashed
ice cold brine up six concrete steps and out
behind the backs of men with the rustle
of Saturday morning racing guides
in their hands,
the smell of blood and sawdust and
ziinnnging of bones being sawn through
in my ears and nose as I went
to empty the bucket across the road, a
look both ways on my way back
to tell the butcher if I had or hadn't
seen the cop; my re-entry to the shop
an important point as I continued on
down the steps, back and forth, the bath
draining low, the morning petering out,
the men, talk abating as the scratchings
were announced on the radio, helped themselves
to a glass of port, disappeared in turn
inside the cool room with the butcher, a notebook
and pencil in his hand; the 10 bob I got
paid telling me butchering was a good way
of life, the note taken from a wad
thick enough to choke a horse.

In the back room at Norm's

The bare floorboards thumped and sprang up
under the boots of yelling and laughing
men come in with the smells of farms,
timber mills and clay mines in their clothes;
their tongues plough shares,
sawblades, sticks of TNT that furrowed, cut
and blasted our boyish ears with tales
that bound our flesh tight about our bones,
as we sat about on benches, backs
to walls hung with photographs of men
with the history of the town in their eyes.

In the centre of the room, Norm
squinted through wire rimmed spectacles,
now and again rocking back on his heels
adding his thoughts to rowdy debates, good-natured
jibes, opinions as he worked his way in grey
pin striped trousers, waistcoat with white shirt-
sleeves held in place by silver armbands, round
a customer's hairy scalp, maintaining his sense of
concentration with pursed lips and a high hat,
clippers, comb and scissors.

A tall, almost elegant figure in the reek
of pipe and cigarette smoke, language tamed
  "in front
of the boys," brush of talc across a fresh
shaven neck, shake of the sheet from out
under a chin as the next stood, crossed
to sit under his hands on the wooden stool
from out the muscle of merriment, warm
as the glow of a lamp, that circled the room.

Forest worker

Purple bell-shaped toadstools
become remarkable in the yellowing
needles on the forest floor,
orange fungi like lanterns lighting
the darkness of rotting wood.

In the gloom of winter
webs glisten like small chandeliers.
Redbreasts sing as the seasons
swing their moods mid-summer
heat spiders relish.

Fresh cut tree stumps glaze
over, glistening and sticky. Wither
and vanish. Witchetty grubs burrow
and wing-it in beetle formation.
Wind snoops around – blows through . . .

A man skins a stick
with his thumbnail, the bark
curling down inside his palm,
the thin white wood split
to nonchalantly pick his teeth.

Then he stands as restlessness
reminds him of his task,
the chainsaw's engine scattering
these thoughts as he goes
crushing toadstools with his boots.

Vic

Arms filled with the ease. The
excitement; daring promoted by fingers
turned traitor to our honest natures,
we struggled in through the door,
empty bottles clinking and slipping
from our grasps.

At first he smiled from his height
above the counter. Handed us the lollies
bulging out two white paper bags
with no hint of suspicion. Smidgin
of reluctance in his fingers.
Clue he was on to us.

A red bandanna of shame went
round our temples, and knotted tight
over our eyes, but we weren't blind
to the rewards. To the signals
those empty bottles sent us outside
the shop's back step.

The links of the chain became links of
iron disappointment threaded through our
sensibilities, the night he padlocked the gate
shut. Reply to his question, "When am I going to
stop buying my own bottles?"

The fizzle of sherbet
making mute our tongues.

When Murray whistled

It was the music of a man
happy with his life, up there
in his garden of vegetables
above the town's main street.

And if you heard the tune,
fingers heavy with your shopping bag,
heart troubled by the personals,
the melody lightened your load.

Hanging washing that pegged
unhappy thoughts to the line,
miserable in the shed, his song
lifted your spirits like a tonic & gin.

A man in a knotted handkerchief,
big square shoulders and hands,
fingers in the rich black soil
among his melons and cauliflowers.

A scarecrow of unpleasantness
out there with the whirligigs and
spinning propellor blades, cut and
nailed to posts just for fun.

It made the town a better place,
men whistling in the streets. Murray
up there like a weather vane
on top of the town's roof.

First love

We met across the handlebars
of our bikes, near the crossroads
halfway down George Street, opposite
Saint Peters, the late-afternoon sunlight
through the tops of the pine trees lining
the Church yard fence. The air cool,
disturbed only by the sound of birds scrabbling to roost.
The occasional thud of a pine cone
landing in the grass. Woodsmoke gushing chimneypots.
Smell of cooking drifting through the town.

I couldn't sleep without thinking about her.
She couldn't sleep without thinking about me.
We wrote each other a letter the very next day.
Signed the very same way.
I LOVE YOU   I LOVE YOU   I LOVE YOU

We saw each other every night.
Learnt the words to all the new songs.
Wrote them down
and sung them out
believing they were written just for us.

We never went further
than holding hands.
Kissing in the grass. Going for walks
in the scrub with a picnic lunch.

Riding our bikes with the wind in our eyes.

For PG

We used to sing those 60s hits
in the back of the old highschool bus,
pussy red pimples on our cheeks,
hair greased into a wave
a mile off Moana beach.

Class time was like doing time,
our hearts outside in our father's world
away from the boredom of books.
(When we could we used to nick off
 to the shops in his little blue Ford.)

What fun we had in that!
Like the time eight of us squeezed inside
off to the drive-in one Friday night,
Barossa Pearl under the seat,
Shorty crammed inside the boot.

The last time I saw him
was just before he died
from the accident in his ute.
We laughed about that old green bus.
Joked about the silly things we used to do.

Like the fight we had in front of the school.
Funny how skun knuckles,
mixed with the taste of sweat and blood,
made us closer then.
Like now, writing you these words.

"Squasha"

was 6'5 and 20 stone
and could customise a car
in 30 minutes
with an axe:

he was 13
when he swapped a transistor radio
for the clapped out old Vanguard
he ran on kero
"flogged" from his father:

by the time he was 16
25 wrecked cars lined "the circuit"
running between the chook-house and dunny
under the clothes-line (regardless of washing)
and round the house (regardless of people):

in between "spinouts"
(once we knocked the dunny over
 with his dad inside)
he gave me cigarettes
and taught me to drive:

now
when I pass by in my comfortable car
thinking uncomfortable thoughts
and spot him bent over
the motor of his favourite "Cusso"

smoke curls upwards
against a sunlit windscreen
and I smell the oil on his fingers
reaching for the gears
as the old Vanguard roars to life . . .

the laughter of our youth
ringing in my ears.

At the pin-ball parlour

He ran yelling out to me
in his grey school-boy uniform,
the words and the sound of his voice
faded now in my memory's ear,
but the sight of him, his eyes
bright with life, haunts the shadows
of my mind.

Hard to believe or understand
that those school-boy shoes
raising healthy dust in the street
as their soles slapped hard on the
hard footpath, were on their way
to a rendezvous with blood
down the barrel of a gun.

I gave his daughter a handful
of twenty cents to play a game. Said
I'd gone to school with her father.
She showed me the tattoo
on her shoulder. A tiger's head
with DAD – Rest in Peace. Shot
a 100,000 with just one ball.

Picking grapes

Time is measured by the quickness
of bunches cut and landing
inside rusty tin buckets.
Slow drone of an aircraft overhead.
Circling of crows.
Laughter of kookaburras far off . . .
Blue heat.
Rustle of green leaves. Rise, drift
and settle of dust from the hurry
of our boots along the row.
Stop/start travel of the tractor
and trailer in tow.
Empty of buckets into the bin.
Turns at the water bag

until

shadows of late-afternoon get inside
the cut of the snips. Fingers opening
and squeezing shut the blades.
Corners of lips. Our eyes,
the long hours beginning to leave
from the bend of our backs,
the day turned the smell of sweat.
Skin stained with juice and dirt.
Men, women and boys reunited
with a sense of who they are,

the taste of our accomplishment
in bottles of wine, dry and sweet.

Milking cows

Pass me the handle of that axe
and I'll gladly chop you a heap of wood.
Bucket to pick up stones out in the far paddock.
Bale to feed through the hammer-mill rather than
go near the bulk of cows in the milking shed.

Perhaps it's the memory of a heifer
I saw be de-horned by fencing wire? Trapped
hooves violent and powerless. A powerlessness that
engulfed me, standing there in the schoolyard
watching barbs of wire redden with blood. Terror
fill soft brown eyes. Moans of a human kind
out that desperate throat.

In the sound of five o'clock news on the radio,
rubber boots on cold cement, dogs slip away out
into the darkness. A procession of dairy cows
follows, stumbling at first, udders swaying
as they raise their great heads, hot vapour
trails clinging to mouths wet with dew.

Their clumsy heaviness approaches.
I'm up here at the chopping block, or else
scrubbing out milk cans. Fuelling the tractor as
something disentangles itself from my logic.
Something dark and brutal that tramples
my reason. Crushes me with fear.

Forking silage

The tines were long and slender.
Each one curved to an alluring point. Sleek
rounded steel prongs polished by the
efforts of our work. The friction of our jab
and heave through fodder flung from the
gleaming tips as we bent our backs to fill
the feeder bins
                    our torsos wet with sweat
                    in the hot sunset.

Thrust, jab and heave went the tines
in rhythm with our thoughts, dulling
the danger of distance closing
between our boots, and those sharp points
skimming the red air between us
like stones skipping over the surface tension
of a pool
                until the waves swallow them up
                like skin closing over a wound.

1966. with a pocketful of dollars and cents

For months I'd been disassociating myself
from the hills. From the people in the streets,
their everyday attire and familiar routines.
Feel of the wind and way the sun shone.
Nights when the moon filled the sky.
Smell of the dew wet grass at dawn. Smoke
in the town's chimney pipes.

Shopkeepers and friends from school. Gates
and fence posts that sign posted my earliest memories.
Doors of houses and rooms where I'd learnt
the lives of my relatives. From my own
family. Comfort given me by my bed
under the side windowsill.

Shadows that drew round me from the corners of
the bedroom, like anxious whispers as I woke to leave.

15 years old
I boarded the bus alone, mum's kiss
wiped on the sleeve of my shirt. Dad's handshake
brushed from my fingers down the leg of my pants.
Brother's back turned to me in his bed, his own
life to live.
I held my head up; kept my shoulders and back straight.

Through the windows
I saw the town recede.
The driver turned the radio on.
I tapped my foot to the beat of the song.

Wakefield Press has been publishing good Australian books
for over fifty years. For a catalogue of current and
forthcoming titles, or to add your name to our mailing list,
send your name and address to

Wakefield Press, Box 2266, Kent Town, South Australia 5071.

TELEPHONE (08) 8362 8800 FAX (08) 8362 7592
WEB www.wakefieldpress.com.au